FORGOTTEN TIMES

THE BRITISH ISLES IN THE 1950s AND 1960s

ALLAN HAILSTONE

AMBERLEY

First published 2025

Amberley Publishing
The Hill, Stroud
Gloucestershire, GL5 4EP

www.amberley-books.com

ISBN: 978 1 3981 2135 5 (print)
ISBN: 978 1 3981 2136 2 (ebook)

British Library Cataloguing in Publication Data.
A catalogue record for this book is available from
the British Library.

Typeset by Simon and Sons ITES Services Pvt. Ltd.,
Chennai, India
Origination by Amberley Publishing.
Printed in the UK.

Appointed GPSR EU Representative: Easy Access
System Europe Oü, 16879218
Address: Mustamäe tee 50, 10621, Tallinn, Estonia
Contact Details: gpsr.requests@easproject.com,
+358 40 500 3575

Introduction

On a typical Sunday morning in 1950, an eleven-year-old urchin might have been seen wandering the streets of a war-devastated Coventry, aiming his box camera at what remained of his home city. He would later return home and attempt to develop the film, then he would make prints from the shots he thought worth keeping.

That urchin remains a familiar figure to me; those were my first efforts to capture pictures of the world around me. The years passed, and in 1955 my father bought me an Agfa Silette 35 mm camera, which I used for many decades including to take most of the photographs in these pages. At school in Coventry, I surreptitiously captured several hundred scenes both in and out of the classroom. I was never caught.

In the 1950s I made several trips to London before finally settling there in 1957 after being accepted at London University. While living in London, on most weekends I would select a city to visit and photograph on a day trip. Two of the more adventurous outings were to Edinburgh and Dublin.

Bablake School, Coventry, 12 May 1954
Bablake School was governed by the universally feared headmaster, Mr Seaborne. The penalty for talking during morning assembly was mandatory: a caning. The penalty for bringing a camera to school and surreptitiously taking photographs during class was not specified.

In almost all cases I tried to note the date and the location. I had noticed that very few photographers seemed to record dates, meaning that all too often people are left to speculate about the date and/or location it was taken.

In this book are just a few of the many hundreds of photographs I took on my sojourns around the British Isles. At the time it did not occur to me that these shots would be seen by anyone more than fifty years later. I also did not appreciate at the time that in future years the interest would lie in how things had changed. Consequently, I should not have taken so many sterile photographs of famous buildings; I should have concentrated more on photographing people and what they were wearing, cars and buses, trolleybus wires, bomb sites and buildings due for demolition. Luckily, however, I took so many shots that many of them do include these things. For this book, I have tried to select images that illustrate how the British Isles have changed over the years.

I hope these photographs will provide a pleasurable and nostalgic lookback to those who have lived in these islands over the years documented, and also give the younger generation a glimpse of a land they never knew.

Coventry, the Godiva Statue Before Its Unveiling, *c.* October 1949
My introduction to photography began with this image. It was taken by me at the age of ten during one of my regular Sunday morning jaunts with my box camera into my home town of Coventry. It depicts the Godiva statue in Broadgate, the central square of the reconstructed city centre, before its unveiling in October 1949. The photograph may even be unique as, during the many years I lived in Coventry, I have never seen another.

Leicester Square, London, 11 April 1955
These two cinemas dominated the north side of Leicester Square, the square that still dominates London's cinema world. The Monseigneur News Theatre was one of several so-called news theatres that ran a continuous performance of cartoons, lasting about an hour at a low price. They no longer exist.

Coventry, the Precinct Under Construction, 16 May 1955

In the mid-1950s work began on clearing the war damage of Coventry's city centre and redeveloping it using the innovative idea of a shopping street free of vehicular traffic. Smithford Street was slightly realigned and named 'the Precinct'. This gave rise to the now universally used term 'shopping precinct'.

Billy Eckstine at the Coventry Hippodrome, 24 May 1955

The Coventry Hippodrome (renamed later that year as the Coventry Theatre) was the principal venue of the city for visiting entertainers. Billy Eckstine was at the time a renowned 'Top Twenty' vocalist, his partnership with the jazz artist Sarah Vaughan being particularly memorable.

Sutton Coldfield, Warwickshire, 30 May 1955
At this time Sutton Coldfield was a town several miles north of Birmingham and functioned as an independent conurbation. It was later incorporated into Birmingham City Council for administrative purposes.

Coventry, Hearsall Common Fair, 4 June 1955
The funfair at Hearsall Common each year was greatly looked forward to by the children of this Midlands city. Less popular for the youngsters was the nearby 'crock fair', founded in 1145, to which the poor mites were dragged by parents more interested in picking up some cheap homewares.

Walsall, Staffordshire, 19 June 1955
Walsall on a wet Sunday afternoon, with the Salvation Army playing in the background. There may have been more interesting places to photograph, but on this occasion it seems I did not find them.

Coventry, the Precinct Under Construction, 13 July 1955
Another image of the construction of the Precinct – two months after that on an earlier page. The section in the background was completed a considerable time after the foreground area was opened. Vehicles were still allowed into the far section, which was still regarded as Smithford Street.

Coventry, Broadgate, 13 July 1955

Broadgate, the main square of Coventry, the location of the Godiva statue and Owen Owen store depicted on earlier pages. When this image was published in a local newspaper in 2018, sixty-three years after I took it, the little girl in the picture contacted me. She still lived in Coventry, and, coincidentally, was living in the same street in which I was born.

London, Strand, 1 August 1955

Strand, more commonly referred to as 'the Strand', is so named from the old use of the word as a reference to the bank of a river. The word also exists with this meaning in the German language. At one time, the Thames lay close to the southern side of this thoroughfare, seen here on the right. The Tivoli Theatre on the right was demolished in 1957. The Vaudeville Theatre opposite can be seen to be running *Salad Days*, which opened in August 1954 and ran for 2,283 performances, at that time the longest-running show in music hall history.

London, Strand, 1 August 1955

Prominent in this image is the Gaiety Theatre, with its cupola. The theatre opened in 1864 as the Strand Musick Hall and closed in 1939, being demolished the year after I took this photograph. In the distance are St Mary-le-Strand and Clement Danes churches.

London, Shaftesbury Avenue, 1 August 1955

When I posted this image on my Twitter feed, the musician Cat Stevens contacted me to ask if I could supply a high-resolution image for his use. At the time I took the photograph he was living at the Moulin Rouge restaurant, owned by his dad. This depicts the northern end of Shaftesbury Avenue, well away from the more well-known theatre end.

London, St Giles High Street, 1 August 1955

One of the lost streets of London's West End. Only a vestige of this section remains. The skyscraper Centre Point now stands in this location. As far as I have been able to determine, my photograph is the only surviving close-up image remaining of this section of the street.

London, Charing Cross Road, 1 August 1955

This view of Charing Cross Road looks north from a vantage point south of Cranbourn Street. Wyndham's Theatre, on the right, displays a flag advertising *The Boy Friend*. The Sandy Wilson musical opened here early in 1954 and ran for five years, one of the longest runs in London theatre history at the time.

London, Trafalgar Square and Strand, 1 August 1955
This looks eastwards from Trafalgar Square. The paw of one of the four Landseer lion statues can be seen on the extreme left, behind which is South Africa House, later the South African Embassy.

London, High Holborn, 2 August 1955
The junction of High Holborn and Kingsway, looking eastwards towards the City (financial) district. To Londoners it will always be regarded as Holborn, despite recent attempts to have it rebranded as trendy 'Midtown'.

London, the Euston Arch, 2 August 1955

This much-lamented arch stood at the entrance to the old Euston station, redeveloped in the early 1960s. It was built in 1837 and demolished in late 1961, despite many protests. Plans to have it reconstructed, partly from the original materials, have so far comes to naught.

Elmdon (Birmingham) Airport, 8 August 1955

Now a major international airport, Birmingham Airport was then termed Elmdon Airport, a small operation alongside the Coventry to Birmingham road serving only Paris, followed shortly afterwards in the late 1950s by services to a small number of Continental cities. This small terminal building was augmented by more terminal buildings in the 1960s. The aircraft shown was a BEA flight about to depart for Paris.

Coventry, the Precinct, *c.* October 1955

Shops in the newly opened Precinct, the precursor to the now universally accepted idea of customers being able to shop well away from vehicular traffic. It is difficult to imagine today how extraordinary this concept felt at the time.

London, Soho, 5 November 1955

The eastern end of Old Compton Street, arguably the centre of activity of this lively area of central London. At this time Soho was a centre of crime and prostitution, and it was advisable not to enter it alone at night. Nowadays it is a tourist area, and far safer to walk around alone at night than many provincial British cities.

London, Charing Cross Road, 5 November 1955

Now a vestige of its former self, Charing Cross Road in the 1950s was a Mecca for lovers of books. Bookshops proliferated throughout its length, from the junction with Oxford Street to Leicester Square. This is a typical example on the eastern side, south of Cambridge Circus. Further along Collets can be seen, the communist-inclined establishment, where one could buy Pravda for 1 penny, the cheapest newspaper available at that time.

London, Cambridge Circus, 5 November 1955

Cambridge Circus lies halfway down Charing Cross Road, at its intersection with Shaftesbury Avenue. Its principal building is the Palace Theatre, off-camera to the left. Marks and Company, the bookshop immortalised in Helene Hanff's novel *84 Charing Cross Road*, is on the far corner behind the main traffic pole. The Circus was the fictional location of the British Intelligence Service in the novels of John le Carre, who termed the organisation 'the Circus'.

The Royal Visit to Coventry, 23 March 1956

On 23 March 1956, Queen Elizabeth and Prince Philip visited Coventry to lay the foundation stone for the new cathedral. Many turned out for the day, as seen here outside the Owen Owen store in Broadgate.

London Pavilion Cinema, 30 July 1956

The London Pavilion cinema and theatre, facing Piccadilly Circus, opened in 1885 as a music hall venue. It became a cinema in 1934 and hosted many major films until its closure in 1985. The film *Rock Around the Clock* was released in 1956, starring the rock and roll band Bill Haley and His Comets, which was a sensational act in the popular music world of the mid-1950s, causing much disturbance during the performances.

London, Piccadilly Circus, 3 January 1957

The 'Monico site' on the north side of Piccadilly Circus. The golden age of illuminated night advertising, before the onset of flat screens and electronic wizardry. Arguably the most well-known was the Guinness Clock, seen here in its first incarnation before it was replaced in 1958 by a somewhat more garish version.

Coventry, the Precinct, 13 April 1957
The Precinct is now almost completed. Beyond the Marks & Spencer building, in what became known as the Lower Precinct, can be seen vestiges of the old Smithford Street, one of the lost streets of the medieval city devastated in the war.

Blackpool, South Shore, 22 April 1957

Blackpool is a predominantly working-class holiday resort on the north-west coast of England. Its most prominent landmark is Blackpool Tower, which opened in 1894 in imitation of the Eiffel Tower in Paris, built a few years earlier. At the time it was the tallest structure in the British Empire. Since the advent of cheap air travel, the town's economy has suffered, not least because of the somewhat inclement weather, but it remains an attractive holiday destination for many of its faithful devotees.

Blackpool, 22 April 1957

Blackpool was, and remains, a magnet for children, and its attractions for youngsters are arguably unrivalled in the British Isles. They include the Pleasure Beach, Zoo, Madame Tussauds, the heritage tramway system, the annual Blackpool lights, and much more.

Leeds Castle, Kent, 24 April 1957

Leeds Castle in 1957 was owned by Lady Olive Baillie, who attempted to keep its existence secret and did not allow those who did not work for her anywhere near. It was then largely unknown, except by locals, but could just be glimpsed through dense woodland from the A20 if one knew exactly where to look. It had, however, appeared in several films, notably *Kind Hearts and Coronets, Sea Devils, Moonraker* and *Waltz of the Toreadors*, but always anonymously or under a false name (Chalfont Castle in *Kind Hearts and Coronets*). Lady Baillie died in 1974 and left the castle to a charitable trust. It is now open to the public.

London Celebrities, 1 August 1957

It is not uncommon to see well-known faces in London, although they are notably absent from Oxford Street. Turn the corner into Bond Street, or go to outlying areas such as Barnes or Hampstead, and they are there in abundance. I managed to photograph these two on the same day. Robin Day, caught in an unguarded moment in Kingsway, changed the face of interviewing. Before he caused a sensation with his incisive cross-examination of Nasser of Egypt, interviewees were asked if they would be kind enough to make a statement. Jack Warner was best known for playing 'Dixon of Dock Green'.

Brighton, *c.* August 1957

Brighton is a vibrant south coast resort easily reached from London by fast trains. A centre for arts and culture following earlier promotion by King George IV, who as regent built the Brighton Pavilion, it has attracted many creative individuals to work and live here. The 'Lanes' and the area known as 'North Layne' are home to a remarkably diverse number of shops and restaurants.

Brighton, *c.* August 1957

This is one of the elegant squares facing the sea between Brighton and Hove, its near neighbour. Sir Laurence Olivier and Vivien Leigh were living here during this period. In 1970, following the withdrawal of kippers from the menu on the *Brighton Belle*, the non-stop Pullman train service to London, Olivier led a successful campaign to have them restored; however, the *Brighton Belle* was discontinued shortly afterwards. Olivier's opinion on this is not recorded. If it had been, it may not have warranted publication here.

London, St James's Theatre, 3 August 1957

St James's Theatre on the south side of King Street after its final performance in July 1957. The theatre hosted the first performance of Oscar Wilde's *The Importance of Being Earnest* in 1895. After the announcement that the theatre would be demolished in favour of an office block, a sizeable campaign was initiated, led by the actress Vivien Leigh, who made an impromptu speech from the public gallery of the House of Lords. The campaign was unsuccessful, and the theatre was demolished in December 1957.

Sudbury, Suffolk, 4 August 1957

Sudbury is a small market town in Suffolk. Its most notable claim to fame is that it is the birthplace of the artist Thomas Gainsborough, and a museum devoted to his work exists in the town. A more gruesome relic is the skull of Simon Sudbury, Archbishop of Canterbury, which is preserved in St Gregory's Church. Sudbury was beheaded in the Tower of London during the Peasants' Revolt of 1381.

London, Charlie Gracie, 5 August 1957

Charlie Gracie (1936–2022) was a major rhythm and blues artist at the time, said to have influenced the Beatles, and topped the bill at the London Hippodrome during that week. In a street off Charing Cross Road, I chanced upon him posing for what later became one of his main promotional images (note his photographer on the right). A few years before his death he saw my photograph on a photographic website and exclaimed: 'Wow, look at all that hair!'.

Above and overleaf: Stonehenge, Wiltshire, 25 May 1958

In the 1950s, the public were not kept well away from Stonehenge, as now, and were free to walk amongst the stones. On the day I visited, work was being done to re-position some stones which had fallen out of their original location, and I was lucky to be able to capture a record of some of this work. On seeing some of my photographs on a website, a few conspiracy theorists have posted their beliefs that Stonehenge is only a few decades old. The same individuals also seem to believe that the moon landings were faked.

Hastings, Sussex, 27 May 1958

Hastings is a resort on the south coast of England, famous for its connection with the Norman invasion and the Battle of Hastings in 1066, although this took place at the location now termed Battle some miles to the north. This image depicts the much-lamented memorial clock tower, commemorating Albert, the Prince Consort. It was built in 1862 after Albert's death, but demolished in 1973 following an arson attack, although it had been under threat for some time because of designs for a new traffic scheme.

Taunton, Somerset, 27 July 1958

Taunton, the county town of Somerset, has much historical significance, dating back to the eighth century. Taunton Castle was built in the tenth century, and a later edifice was built by the Normans after the invasion. Significant events of the Wars of the Roses also occurred at Taunton.

Minehead, Somerset, 27 July 1958

Minehead is a coastal town in Somerset, in the south-west of England. Boasting a fine sandy beach, it is a popular holiday resort for families. The most picturesque area is arguably Church Steps, seen here during a rainstorm, and leading to St Michael's Church, from which there are fine views.

Cardiff, 28 July 1958

Located within a few miles of the sea in South Wales, Cardiff is both the capital of Wales and its largest city. The British Empire and Commonwealth Games were being held in Cardiff in 1958, which accounts for the statue on the top of the Howells department store in these shots of St Mary Street.

Cardiff, 28 July 1958

As a continuation of St Mary Street, High Street (seen here) leads to Cardiff Castle. The original motte-and-bailey castle (not in this shot but behind the front façade) was built in the late eleventh century. Further additions were made until comparatively recently. The castle is now a tourist attraction open to the public.

Above and opposite: Bristol, 30 July 1958

Bristol is the largest city in south-west England and lies in a strategic position near where the River Severn widens to become the Bristol Channel. A major centre of communications and a hub for creative talent, its importance cannot be overstated. Clifton, with its famous suspension bridge over the River Avon, built to an early design by Brunel, is an area especially associated with creativity and artistic work of all types. Its many devotees will agree with the accolades it has received as the best place to live in Britain.

Bristol, St Peter's Church, 30 July 1958
St Peter's Church stands on the site of Bristol's first church (twelfth century). Additions were made to the church foundations over future centuries, but in 1940 the church was heavily bombed in the Blitz, and it is now maintained as a memorial to those Bristolians killed in the war.

Above and opposite: Folkestone, 2 August 1958
Folkestone lies on the coast at the south-east corner of Kent and is a major port for Channel crossings. It is also near the entrance to the Channel Tunnel. Charles Dickens had an affection for Folkestone, in particular Old High Street, shown here, and lived in the town around 1855.

Brompton, Gillingham, Kent, 3 August 1958

Fast disappearing from the High Street are these privately owned establishments, often termed 'corner shops', with their improvised signage and owners who knew their regular customers and their wants. Competition from supermarkets, who can buy goods in bulk at lower prices, has hastened their demise.

Aylesford, Kent, 3 August 1958

Aylesford is a picturesque village on the River Medway, 4 miles from Maidstone. Many Iron Age and Bronze Age artefacts have been discovered in the vicinity. Aylesford Bridge, built of Kentish ragstone, was built in the fourteenth century and was one of the earliest crossing points over the Medway.

Maidstone, Kent, 3 August 1958

Maidstone is the largest town in Kent and the county town, lying on the River Medway. Notable buildings include Leeds Castle, some miles to the east, and the fourteenth-century Archbishop's Palace on the banks of the Medway. The enormous Mote Park, in the centre of the town, is considerably larger than London's Hyde Park.

Mote Park, Maidstone, Kent, 3 August 1958

Harry Secombe makes his way back to the Pavilion, one of several familiar faces taking part in a Sunday afternoon charity match in Mote Park, Maidstone. He appears none too happy with his fate that day.

Canterbury, Kent, 4 August 1958

The classic view along the medieval Mercery Lane, leading to Buttermarket and the cathedral. Originally La Mercerie, in olden times it was lined with shops selling merchandise to pilgrims on their way to the tomb of Thomas Becket.

Canterbury, Kent, 4 August 1958

The western end of High Street, leading to the fourteenth-century Westgate, the largest gatehouse in England and one of the best preserved. Built of Kentish ragstone, in the medieval period it served as the principal entrance to the city from London. It now houses a museum.

Margate, Kent, 4 August 1958

Margate is a popular seaside resort on the extreme north-east coast of Kent, noted for the Dreamland Amusement Park and its sandy beaches, attracting many families with children using the excellent transport links.

Tenterden, Kent, 5 August 1958

Tenterden is a small town near Ashford, founded in the fourteenth century as a result of the wool industry. St Mildred's Church arose from twelfth-century foundations, with the tower being added in 1461, and is named after St Mildred, a seventh-century princess.

Rye Station, East Sussex, 5 August 1958

Rye lies about halfway along the Ashford to Hastings railway line. Rye is a small but remarkably picturesque town that was originally one of the Cinque Ports but is now 2 miles from the sea. It has been the location chosen for a number of television and film dramas, and records show it as a settlement as early as the Roman occupation.

Above and overleaf: Ashford, Kent, 5 August 1958

Ashford, at this time a small town on the main road from London to the Channel-crossing ports of Dover and Folkestone, was subsequently considerably redeveloped, though not without controversy. A major innovation was the opening of Ashford International station, a stopping point on the Eurostar high-speed Channel Tunnel services between London and Paris/Brussels. The stopping of trains at Ashford on this service was suspended in 2023, but the line continues to provide a high-speed rail service to London with a journey time of thirty-eight minutes.

SERCOMBE'S
MANS SHOP
THE SCHOOL SHOP
SERCOMBES

Kodak
FILM
Imperial
Typewriters

High Street, Slough, Berkshire, 23 October 1958

Slough, a small town in Berkshire near Windsor, is notable for the defamatory John Betjeman poem (which he later regretted) and for Slough Trading Estate, incorporating the highest number of companies outside London. It has undergone considerable redevelopment in recent years.

Cowes, Isle of Wight, 26 October 1958

The Isle of Wight lies off the southern coast of mainland Britain, and Cowes is a gateway town on the northern coast of the island, linked to Southampton by passenger ferry. Much of the industry of the town is linked to marine craft.

Edinburgh, 1 November 1958

Two views looking westwards along Princes Street, the main street of the area known as the new town. The 61-metre Scott Monument, to the left, is a Victorian edifice dedicated to the writer Sir Walter Scott and stands in Princes Street Gardens. It has never been cleaned because of possible damage to the stone.

Edinburgh, 1 November 1958
The view of Princes Street looking eastwards. On the right of the street, the Scott Monument, and beyond it the tower with the clock, belongs to the North British Hotel (now the Balmoral Hotel). In the far distance are the monuments on Calton Hill.

Faversham, Kent, 6 December 1958
Faversham is a small market town near the north Kent coast, known for its picturesque appearance, notably in Abbey Street, and its historical connections. Lying on the Roman road of Watling Street, the settlement was established before the Roman occupation and throughout its history has been the beneficiary of a number of royal privileges and charters.

Royal Tunbridge Wells, Kent, 24 January 1959

The Pantiles, a colonnade of shops and other establishments, is the best-known feature of this attractive town. The area dates from the seventeenth century, after the discovery of iron-rich spring water nearby, and was originally termed 'the Walks', and later 'the Parade'. It has often been used as a filming location in cinema and television productions.

Dublin, Republic of Ireland, 31 January 1959

One of my more adventurous weekends took me to Dublin, the capital of the Republic of Ireland. My main impression was of stepping back in time and of the enormous amount of litter in the streets. I knew how Dorothy felt in *The Wizard of Oz* when she said, 'I've a feeling we're not in Kansas anymore.'

Dublin, Republic of Ireland, 31 January 1959

O'Connell Bridge, viewed here from the south side, spans the River Liffey and leads to O'Connell Street on the north bank. The bridge was built as Carlisle Bridge between 1791 and 1794, being widened and renamed around 1880.

Dublin, Republic of Ireland, 31 January 1959

The post office on the left played an important role during the Easter Rising of 1916. Nelson's Pillar, built in 1809, was spectacularly blown up on 8 March 1966, possibly by Republican elements in celebration of the fiftieth anniversary of the Rising.

Dublin, Republic of Ireland, 31 January 1959

The view of O'Connell Street from the top of Nelson's Pillar, looking south towards O'Connell Bridge.

Middle Abbey Street, Dublin, Republic of Ireland, 31 January 1959
'In Dublin's fair city...' I think she relished being photographed.

Dublin, Republic of Ireland, 31 January 1959
I came across this waif while looking around for items to photograph. Presumably laws about minimum age for employment were somewhat lax.

Windsor, Berkshire, 19 May 1959

Windsor Bridge, opened in 1824, links Eton and Windsor. Windsor Castle, originally built by William the Conqueror as a motte-and-bailey castle in the eleventh century, was expanded in later centuries and is now one of the principal royal residences. It suffered a disastrous fire in 1992.

Liverpool, Royal Liver Building, 18 June 1959

The 104-metre Royal Liver Building stands at Liverpool's pierhead and is the city's iconic and most well-recognised landmark. It was opened in 1911 as the headquarters of the Royal Liver Insurance Group, later assimilated into the Royal London Group. The clock tower is now open to the public.

Port St Mary, Isle of Man, 19 June 1959

Port St Mary, once a fishing port, lies near the southern end of the Isle of Man, an island in the Irish Sea that is a self-governing dependency and not part of the United Kingdom. It is a tourist destination with an attractive sandy beach.

Castletown, Isle of Man, 19 June 1959

Castletown, founded in the eleventh century, was the capital of the Isle of Man until 1869, when this title was transferred to Douglas. This view is from the top of the thirteenth-century Castle Rushen. On the right is the Castletown brewery.

Douglas, Isle of Man, June 1959

One of the principal tourist attractions in Douglas, the capital of the Isle of Man, is the Douglas Bay Horse Tramway, which runs along the seafront promenade. The service began in 1876 and has run almost continuously since then, although some scaling-down has been necessary recently because of financial losses. The system uses over forty horses.

Belfast, 20 June 1959

The aftermath of a disastrous fire in Belfast, the capital and largest city of Northern Ireland, part of the United Kingdom. Throughout its history the city has been a major centre of industry, notably the location of the Harland & Wolff shipyard, where the ill-fated RMS *Titanic* was uilt.

Belfast, 20 June 1959

Donegall Square is the focal point of Belfast city centre, lying at the end of Donegall Place, the main shopping street. It is the location of City Hall (off-camera) and the Scottish Provident Building, seen in this image at the far end of the square. The trolleybuses were phased out in 1968.

Portrush, Northern Ireland, 20 June 1959

Portrush, County Antrim, is a small town on the north coast of Northern Ireland, about 50 miles (80 km) from Belfast. Its three sandy beaches draw many tourists, and the nearby Giant's Causeway is a further attraction.

Breakdown, Isle of Man, 22 June 1959

Although complaints about the state of the railways in the UK are commonplace, this state of affairs is rarely encountered. On my return to the Isle of Man from Northern Ireland, my train broke down in the middle of nowhere and it was decided that any repair was out of the question. The entire train was evacuated and all passengers had to walk along the track to the nearest station.

Lincoln Cathedral, 27 July 1959
At 525 feet (160 metres), Lincoln Cathedral was possibly the tallest building in the world when its central spire was completed in the fourteenth century. However, the spire collapsed in 1548 and was never replaced. Work on the cathedral itself began shortly after the Norman invasion, resulting in one of the finest buildings of its kind in the world. Many historical figures are buried in the cathedral, including Eleanor of Castile.

Lincoln, the Stonebow, 27 July 1959
The Stonebow, the arch over Lincoln High Street, dates from the sixteenth century, although some form of gateway to the city had existed at this spot from Roman times. The building that houses the arch is the Guildhall.

Chipping Campden, Gloucestershire, 12 August 1959

Chipping Campden is a small market town in the Cotswolds area of England, originally a centre for the wool trade. The term 'chipping' derives from the Old English word for market. The town is a centre for tourists, attracted by its picturesque appearance, including the seventeenth-century market hall.

Left and opposite: Evesham, Worcestershire, 12 August 1959
Evesham is a market town in the West Midlands, founded *c*. AD 700 around Evesham Abbey, of which fragments remain and where Lady Godiva is reputedly buried. The town is almost entirely surrounded by the River Avon, making flooding a regular occurrence.

Worcester, 12 August 1959

Worcester, founded on the River Severn in the seventh century, is home to one of England's major cathedrals. Notable industries in the city include Royal Worcester porcelain. Seen here is the much-admired Glover's Needle, which is visible for miles around on account of the flat terrain in the area.

Cowes, Isle of Wight, 16 August 1959

Another shot of Cowes after my first visit in 1958. This is the High Street, host to establishments such as the Fountain Hotel and Pascall Atkey & Son, ship chandlers. Students of banking history will also note the National Provincial Bank.

Southampton, 16 August 1959
Southampton New Docks. I am advised that the ship is the SS *Nevasa*, built in 1955–56.

Southampton, 16 August 1959
The view of Southampton from Mayflower Park. Southampton is a major port on the south coast of England and was the port of departure for the *Titanic* and the *Mayflower*. The city was founded soon after the Roman invasion in the first century owing to its strategic location and was heavily bombed during the Second World War.

Above, below and opposite: Nottingham, 27 August 1959
Nottingham is a major city, sporting and tourist centre in the East Midlands. It is noted for its lace-making industry and is proud of its association with Robin Hood and the stories of his escapades in the nearby Sherwood Forest. Seen here, the domed Council House is the city's most prominent architectural landmark, visible from a considerable distance in all directions.

Lewes, Sussex, 10 October 1959

Lewes, the county town of Sussex, now East Sussex, is a market town of much historical significance, containing several notable buildings such as Lewes Castle. The annual bonfire procession and commemoration of the burning of the martyrs attract much interest. The one-time village of Cliffe, at the far end of the High Street is now assimilated into Lewes itself. The 15th century bookshop, depicted, still exists at the time of writing.

Norwich,
18 October 1959
Norwich is a cathedral city and the county town of Norfolk. A settlement began to be established at the present site around the fifth century, near the Roman settlement of Caistor, the capital of East Anglia. *Top*: The view from Upper King Street along Tombland; *Middle*: Elm Hill, arguably the most picturesque area; *Bottom*: Alongside the River Wensum.

Arundel, Sussex, 8 November 1959

Arundel lies on the River Arun in West Sussex. Its most notable landmark is Arundel Castle, which was built in the eleventh century but much restored after being damaged in the English Civil War. Arundel itself began as a Saxon village and became an important market town under the Normans.

Sheffield, Fitzalan Square, 15 November 1959

Sheffield, a major industrial city in Yorkshire, is famed for its connection with the steel industry. The origins of the settlement are lost to time, but it was long before the Norman invasion. Those who have not visited may assume an image of an uninteresting industrial centre, but I found it a fascinating and lively city with an ambience that needs to be experienced first-hand. This image is of Fitzalan Square, the centre of market activity in the Middle Ages, which was created as a modern square in 1881 and named after the nearby Fitzalan Market Hall. The cinema in the image was destroyed by fire in 1984.

Edinburgh, Princes Street, 17 April 1960

This shot, looking westwards from the eastern end of Princes Street, shows the Scott Monument in Princes Street Gardens and the statue of the Duke of Wellington by Sir John Steell outside Register House on the north side of Princes Street, opposite the North British Hotel (now the Caledonian Hotel).

Edinburgh, Waverley Station, 17 April 1960

Waverley station derived from North Bridge station, opened in 1846, and General station, opened in 1847. These later became known as Waverley station, named after the Waverley novels of Sir Walter Scott. The present station is now the principal one of the city, serving London's Kings Cross and many other destinations. Waverley Steps, at the time a dismal staircase at the side of the station, was later developed as a shopping centre with escalators.

Crossing the Firth of Forth, 17 April 1960

At this time there was no direct road transport across the Forth in the vicinity of Edinburgh, and passengers with vehicles or those unwilling to take the train were reliant, as here, on the ferry service across the Firth of Forth. These images show passengers from South Queensferry awaiting the next ferry, and vehicles awaiting to disembark on the north side.

Forth Rail Bridge, 17 April 1960

The Forth Rail Bridge is a cantilever bridge which opened in 1890. It is also a UNESCO World Heritage Site and the view of it is famous worldwide, as is the myth that painting the bridge never stops. This is the view from North Queensferry. One of my Twitter (now known as X) friends pointed out the tiny pram in the picture, and that the politician Gordon Brown had connections with the village. Unfortunately, the dates did not quite match up.

Forth Rail Bridge, 17 April 1960

The classic view of the Forth Rail Bridge is usually from this vantage point on South Queensferry. This image also shows the ferries of the service known as Queensferry Passage, initiated in the eleventh century but discontinued after the opening of the Forth Road Bridge.

Edinburgh, Princes Street, 17 April 1960

This view eastwards along Princes Street from the north side includes the Scott Monument, the North British Hotel (now the Caledonian Hotel) and, in the far distance, some of the mainly nineteenth-century monuments on Calton Hill. The hotel clock is always kept a few minutes fast, a tradition that dates from when passengers used it to time the departure of their train from the nearby Waverley station.

Edinburgh, Princes Street, 17 April 1960

Princes Street viewed from the vicinity of Edinburgh Castle. Princes Street, the principal thoroughfare of the New Town and its main shopping street, runs west to east between Lothian Road and Leith Street. Originally named Prince's Street (possessive case), after Prince George, later George IV, the apostrophe was later dropped after prolonged colloquial use. The shops lie almost exclusively on the northern side, with the southern side occupied to a large extent by Princes Street Gardens.

Edinburgh Castle, 17 April 1960

At the time of this photograph, sentry guards were stationed around the clock at the entrance to Edinburgh Castle. The hourly changing of the guard was always enjoyed by tourists. Amidst much controversy, the guards were removed from duty in recent years as their presence was considered a waste of resources which could be better occupied elsewhere.

Glasgow, the Tolbooth Steeple, 18 April 1960

Glasgow Tolbooth was built in the seventeenth century at Glasgow Cross, a major intersection point of several streets and hub of activity of old Glasgow. After the building had increasingly fallen into disrepair, the main building was demolished in 1921, leaving only the steeple remaining.

Glasgow, Gorbals, 18 April 1960

Gorbals was known as a notorious slum area on the south bank of the River Clyde, and advice was sometimes given for outsiders not to enter the area. In later years Gorbals was redeveloped a number of times according to prevailing perceptions and has now lost its old reputation.

Glasgow, Trongate, 18 April 1960

Trongate, the eastward continuation of Argyle Street, leads at its eastern end to Glasgow Cross and is one of the city's oldest streets. A notable architectural structure is the steeple of the old Tron Church, most of which was destroyed by fire in 1793. The tram system was discontinued in 1962.

Glasgow, Argyle Street, 18 April 1960

Argyle Street, originally known as Westergait, was renamed in the eighteenth century. It is the longest of the main shopping thoroughfares of the city, running from Trongate in the east, under the railway lines leading out of Glasgow Central station and then westwards out of the city. The passage under the lines is known to Glaswegians as 'Hielanman's Umbrella' and dates from the time when working Highlanders used the area for meetings. The main shops in the street are in the area east of the 'umbrella'.

Above, below and overleaf: Glasgow, Gorbals, 19 April 1960

The principal and overwhelming impression of the Gorbals, then a slum area south of the Clyde, was of streets teeming with children playing a myriad of games and activities. Unlike today, when fearful parents closet their offspring indoors or arrange for them to be closely guarded, children were allowed to roam as and where they pleased. Whether they came to any harm or whether this encouraged a healthy outlook for their future is open to question.

Glasgow, an Illegal Betting Shop, 19 April 1960

I managed to capture this shot by looking behind a door, which I saw suspicious characters furtively entering and leaving from. I was fortunate not to have been spotted, otherwise this and my other Glasgow photographs would probably not have survived. These illegal betting shops were known to exist, but their locations were only known to local punters and they were regularly raided by the police (when they could find them). In later years, betting shops were regulated and legalised.

Glasgow, Aftermath of the Whisky Bond Fire, 19 April 1960

The whisky bond fire in Glasgow's Cheapside Street on the evening of 28 March 1960, one of Glasgow's many fires, was one of the worst experienced, not only in that city, but in the whole of the UK. Nineteen firefighters were killed in the explosion and subsequent collapse of the warehouse.

Glasgow, Argyle Street, 19 April 1960

A No. 26 tram in Argyle Street. This route ran from Burnside to Scotstoun/Dalmuir. It was replaced by a bus service in June 1962 and a few months later the fondly remembered tram service was scrapped altogether.

Glasgow, Argyle Street, 19 April 1960

Argyle Street looking west from near the corner of Union Street on the northern side. The 'SCHWEPPES' sign is at the entrance to the 'Hielanman's Umbrella', the passage under the lines from Glasgow Central station.

Glasgow, Buchanan Street/Argyle Street, 19 April 1960

The view looking north along Buchanan Street from the corner with Argyle Street, with St Enoch Square behind the camera.

Glasgow, Argyle Street, 19 April 1960

This shot of Argyle Street is from the south side, looking east. The corner establishment on the right, Timothy Whites, may help with orientation as it appears in another image in this book taken on the same day. Timothy Whites, a long-established chain of dispensing chemists, was taken over by Boots Pure Drug Company in 1968.

Glasgow, St Enoch Stations, 19 April 1960

St Enoch main line railway station was opened in 1876. With twelve platforms, it ran services to many parts of Scotland and England. It closed in 1966 after the Beeching rail cuts and was demolished in 1977. On the site is now the St Enoch Centre, a shopping centre. The Underground station, also seen here, is a Victorian red sandstone building. It still exists, although not serving its original purpose.

Glasgow, Buchanan Street, 19 April 1960

Now entirely pedestrianised, Buchanan Street is the principal north–south shopping street of the central area of Glasgow, with a greater preponderance of upmarket flagship establishments than Argyle Street and Sauchiehall Street. This view is from the eastern side of the street looking north, at the junction with Argyle Street. Buchanan Street is notable for the extent of its Victorian architecture.

Wellmeadow Street, Paisley, Renfrewshire, 19 April 1960

Paisley was established in the twelfth century and has become well known as a centre of the weaving industry. The Paisley Shawl is renowned worldwide. The town lies around 7 miles (12 km) west of Glasgow.

Glasgow, Argyle Street, 19 April 1960

This view of Argyle Street looks eastwards from a vantage point near St Enoch Square. Lewis's department store (not to be confused with the John Lewis Partnership) was one of a number of large stores in the chain that operated for many years in a small number of provincial cities until 2010. Lewis's store in Birmingham was the only sizeable department store in the city.

**Portsmouth,
30 April 1960**
This view of Portsmouth is from the vessel MV Shanklin, which operated as a passenger ferry to the Isle of Wight until 1980.

Union Street, Ryde, Isle of Wight, 30 April 1960
Ryde lies on the north-east coast of the Isle of Wight and is a gateway to the island for ferries and a hovercraft service from Portsmouth and Southsea. It is noted for its unusually long pier, opened in 1814. The town has many amenities for tourists and is popular as a holiday destination.

**Portsmouth,
30 April 1960**
The University of Portsmouth Park Building and, beyond it, the Guildhall. Portsmouth, a major port on the south coast of England, technically lies not on the mainland but on Portsea Island in the Solent. A settlement nearby was in existence in Roman times. Portsmouth has been a strategic location for defence and naval operations down the centuries.

Speke Airport, Liverpool, 5 May 1960

I took this photograph from an aircraft that had just landed on a flight from London. The airport, originally termed Liverpool (Speke) Airport, started flights in 1930 but was not officially opened until 1933. A few months after I took this photograph plans were drawn up for a major redevelopment. Liverpool John Lennon Airport, as it is now known, is an important hub for many airlines.

Liverpool, 6 May 1960

Liverpool will need no introduction to anyone familiar with the British Isles. A major centre for music and culture, the city possesses numerous galleries, museums and listed buildings. Arguably its most well-known landmark, the Liver Building, with its liver birds, can be seen in this image in the distance. The eagle-eyed may also spot the cinema advertising 'Royal Wedding', presenting the film of the wedding of Princess Margaret three days earlier.

Liverpool, Mersey Tunnel Entrance, 6 May 1960
The Mersey (Queensway) Tunnel shown here, now one of two, opened in 1934, and connects the city of Liverpool with Birkenhead on the opposite side of the Mersey. Now referred to by locals as 'the Old Tunnel', when it opened it was the longest road tunnel in the world.

Chester, Foregate Street, 7 May 1960
Chester is one of the most historic cities in the British Isles. It was founded in the first century AD as a Roman fort, and after the Norman invasion William I built Chester Castle in the south-west of the city, overlooking the River Dee and the Welsh border. The city walls are amongst the best preserved of any in England. Depicted is one of the principal sights of Chester: the Eastgate clock, which stands on the gate through the city walls.

Chester, Eastgate Street, 7 May 1960

The continuation of Foregate Street beyond
the city wall in the previous image is Eastgate
Street. This image was taken from a vantage
point on the city wall near the Eastgate clock.
At the time of this photograph road traffic
dominated the city centre, but nowadays
much of the city centre, including Eastgate
Street, is largely pedestrianised.

Chester Cathedral, 7 May 1960

Chester Cathedral, a Grade I listed building,
was first inaugurated in the tenth century on
or near the site of a Christian basilica which
existed during the Roman occupation. Over
the centuries it was extensively modified
and restored, and this is reflected in the
several architectural styles now apparent
in the structure. The bell tower was added
comparatively recently in the twentieth
century. This view is along St Werburgh Street.

Chester, the Rows, 7 May 1960

The Chester Rows are an attractive destination for many visitors to the city. Although one hesitates to use the term 'unique', the Rows are certainly unusual. They consist of a set of first-floor, covered, half-timbered walkways along several streets, with entrances to the establishments in those streets. It is thought that they may date from medieval times. As can be seen here, the Rows are a popular meeting point for shoppers in the city.

Chester Town Hall, 7 May 1960

The imposing Town Hall in Chester's Northgate Street was opened in 1869 by the Prince of Wales, the future Edward VII. Built in grey and red sandstone, its interior is no less impressive than its exterior and is adorned with busts and sculptures.

Wrexham, Brook Street, 7 May 1960

Wrexham, then in Denbighshire, is a Welsh city on the border with Cheshire in England. Although traces of a settlement have been found that date from the Mesolithic era, the present city was founded around the eleventh century. Wrexham later became important as a centre of iron, steel and coal production. Brook Street, seen here, was built above and parallel to the small River Gwenfro, which no doubt accounts for its name.

Wrexham, 7 May 1960

I was intrigued by this bizarre structure
enough to photograph it. In later research
I discovered it was the spire of St Mark's
Church, originally 200 feet tall and the tallest
building in Wrexham. The church closed in
1956 after being found to be structurally
unsafe; the remains were demolished shortly
after this photograph was taken.

Shrewsbury, 7 May 1960

Shrewsbury is the county town of Shropshire,
lying on the River Severn. The town is
renowned for its unspoilt town centre dating
from medieval times and its eleventh-century
sandstone castle, depicted here. Excavations
have revealed a settlement here dating from
the seventh century.

Shrewsbury Station, 7 May 1960

Shrewsbury railway station is of particular interest to railway historians. It was built in 1848/49 in imitation Tudor Gothic style in Grinshill stone, funded by four separate railway companies. The station was rebuilt at the turn of the twentieth century. The town now lies on a somewhat minor route, although there are a limited number of direct trains to London Euston.

York, 26 August 1960

One of the principal tourist attractions in York is (the) Shambles, the narrow historic street containing many medieval buildings dating from the fourteenth century onwards. The name derives from the old name for slaughterhouses and butchers. The street is now home to cafés, boutiques and an open-air market.

York Railway Station, 26 August 1960
York station is a key station on the East Coast Main Line between London Kings Cross and Edinburgh. Although a train service had existed since around 1840, the present station was built in the mid-1870s and when opened was the largest station in the world. This image shows Platform 8 from the footbridge, which was built in 1938.

Durham Cathedral, 27 August 1960
Durham Cathedral lies in an imposing position high above a bend in the River Wear. It was built around 1090 and is now regarded as one of the major cathedrals in the country. It is now a UNESCO World Heritage Site.

Durham, Crossgate, 27 August 1960

The city of Durham was founded by monks from Lindisfarne shortly before the Norman invasion, although some form of settlement appears to have been here from much earlier times. This street, Crossgate, is an ancient street leading west from the city centre to Neville's Cross, from which the street derives its name.

Newcastle-upon-Tyne, Grainger Street, 27 August 1960

Newcastle-upon-Tyne is the most populous city in the north-east of England and requires little introduction. Grainger Street, seen here, is the principal street of the area known as Grainger Town, named after Richard Grainger, who built many of the finest classical buildings in the whole of Newcastle. Grey's Monument, visible at the far end of Grainger Street, was erected in 1838 and commemorates Earl Grey, one-time prime minister. Urban transport historians will note the trolleybus wires; the service was discontinued in 1966.

Tyne Bridge, Newcastle-upon-Tyne/Gateshead, 27 August 1960

Of the (now) seven bridges over the River Tyne between the centres of Newcastle and Gateshead, the most prominent and easily recognised as a symbol of the two cities is known simply as the Tyne Bridge. The single-arch road bridge (known architecturally as a 'through arch bridge') was opened in 1928 and is similar in appearance, though not in size, to Sydney Harbour Bridge, also built by Dorman Long.

Newcastle-upon-Tyne, Central Station, 27 August 1960

Newcastle Central station lies on the East Coast Main Line between London Kings Cross and Edinburgh. The station opened in 1850 in Newcastle's Grainger Town area. The year after this photograph was taken much of the roof was destroyed in a large fire, and in recent years the station has been extensively modernised. Students of inflation will note the advertised fare to London of 52*s* 6*d*, which older readers will be aware converts to £2.62 (plus a decimal halfpenny).

York, 27 August 1960

York, the cathedral city and county town of Yorkshire, was founded as Eboracum by the Romans in the first century. The city walls were originally built around AD 70 and are remarkably well preserved, probably more so than anywhere else in England, although much of the construction dates from the thirteenth century.

York Castle Museum, 27 August 1960

York Castle Museum is an award-winning museum considered as one of the best in the British Isles. Especially memorable is Kirkgate, a reconstructed Victorian street. Each shop on the street is named after a real establishment that existed in York in Victorian times.

York Minster, 27 August 1960

York Minster is one of the world's foremost cathedrals. Founded in the seventh century, it is the seat of the Archbishop of York. After centuries of restoration and further additions, it was completed in the fifteenth century to include a magnificent display of medieval stained glass.

Hull, Paragon Square, 28 August 1960

Kingston-upon-Hull, better known as Hull, is a port city on the River Hull in the East Riding of Yorkshire, though is several miles from the east coast. Hull was extensively damaged during the Second World War and subsequently redeveloped. This location, Paragon Square, is one of the very few locations of the now-defunct 'Guinness Clock' promotion which lasted for many decades.

CND Rally, Trafalgar Square, London, 24 September 1960

This was one of a number of rallies held in Trafalgar Square by CND, the Campaign for Nuclear Disarmament, founded in 1957. Many members advocated unilateral disarmament, whereby the United Kingdom would disarm while other nations, including the Soviet Union, would retain nuclear weapons.

Peel, Isle of Man, 29 August 1961

Peel is a fishing port on the west coast of the Isle of Man, noted for its sandy beach and the ruined Peel Castle on St Patrick's Isle. This connected to Peel via a causeway, from which this image was taken. At one time Peel was the capital of the Isle of Man.

Coventry Cathedral, *c.* April 1962

The original Coventry Cathedral (Church of St Michael) was destroyed in the Blitz on 14 November 1940. It was decided to leave the ruined cathedral as a symbol of the futility of war and to build the new cathedral alongside and at right angles to its predecessor. It was opened on 25 May 1962. In anticipation of the many thousands of photographs destined to be taken of the new cathedral, this is one of a few I took from a slightly different perspective.

Window Display, London, *c.* December 1962

My records of this shot are incomplete, but I recall that I took it somewhere around Regent Street, near Oxford Circus, possibly at Liberty's department store.

Loch an Eilein, Cairngorms National Park, Scotland, 1964

Loch an Eilein ('loch of the island') is a freshwater loch around 3 miles (5 km) south of Aviemore in Cairngorms National Park, Scotland. The fourteenth-century ruined castle, shown here, lies on an island in the middle of the loch. The location has been popular with tourists as a recreation spot for many years.

Forth Road Bridge Under Construction, 8 March 1964

A source of frustration for many years, travellers wishing to take a vehicle across the Firth of Forth in the vicinity of Edinburgh needed to take the car ferry at Queensferry. Plans to build a road bridge were mooted as early as 1947. After final approval, work began on the construction of a suspension bridge in 1958. This was opened on 4 September 1964 and the ferry service at Queensferry was discontinued.

Barra, Outer Hebrides, 14 March 1964

Probably the most bizarre aspect of air travel within the British Isles is the service between Glasgow and the island of Barra in the Outer Hebrides, where the aircraft lands on the beach at Barra. In 1964, the service was operated by BEA (British European Airways), which was later subsumed into British Airways.

Sark, Channel Islands, 22 March 1965

Sark lies in the Channel Islands, the remnants of an ancient duchy off the coast of France; the islands are not part of the United Kingdom. Sark is part of the Bailiwick of Guernsey and has its own laws, including the directive that cars are banned from the island. The principal mode of transport is the tractor. Shown here is the narrow isthmus joining Greater Sark and Little Sark, passage across which can occasionally be perilous owing to high winds. The inhabitants of Little Sark retain a fierce independence, even to the extent of using their own dialect.

About the Author

Allan Hailstone was born in Coventry in 1938 and at the age of ten began photographing street scenes of his war-ravaged home town. On graduating from reading Chemical Engineering at Imperial College in 1960, he worked in the field of patents on metallurgical issues and also constructed a database of auction prices of British coinage. This later led to becoming co-author of two of the principal priced standard catalogues of British and Irish coinage. He continued in his interest of photographing street scenes in many countries throughout the world, amassing an archive of thousands of images. Allan regularly posts selections of these street scenes on Twitter (now X) and welcomes new friends on this platform.

Also by the Author
Berlin in the Cold War: 1959 to 1966 (Amberley Publishing)
London: Portrait of a City, 1950 to 1962 (Amberley Publishing)
Standard Catalogue of English and UK Coins (co-author) (Coincraft)
Standard Catalogue of the Coins of Scotland, Ireland, Channel Islands and Isle of Man
    (co-author) (Coincraft)